The Passion for Radio

Elize Cilliers

Inquiries and Book Orders should be addressed to:

Great Writers Media
Email: info@greatwritersmedia.com
Phone: 877-600-5469

ISBN: 978-1-959493-38-9 (sc)
ISBN: 978-1-959493-37-2 (ebk)

Dedication

To my mother Engela Cilliers who set the pace for writing and passed away much to early.

To my loving husband Kobus which never ever seem to give up, no matter how difficult the task ahead. Without you this book would never have been written.

Love you both.
Elize Cilliers

Contents

Acknowledgments

It seems as if time has passed so quickly, unnoticed by anyone. We feel very fortunate to have walked this path for 14 years. We would like to thank Abba Father for making this dream possible and for strengthening us to fulfill it. Thanks to Hennie and Riana Smit for their encouragement and contributions. This would never have been possible without Hennie's knowledge of Radio and Television.

It is our privilege to thank the listeners from across the globe for their support.

CHAPTER 1

Early Years

Jacobus Cornelius Swanepoel (Here refer to as Kobus), was born in the City of Klerksdorp on a lovely spring day on the 12th September 1956. The suburb was Pienaarsdorp, specific address Kleynhans Street 9. He would become a shy boy but inherit his father's self confidence and business skills.

His father was John William Swanepoel and his mother Johanna Swanepoel. John was a skilled business man as well as a politician. He owned several business. To mention some, caffe's a tyre business as well as a paint business. He later started to build a few houses and sold them. He once painted the city of Klerksdorp's chart.

John was also involved in politics and served on the city of Klerksdorp's board for 26 years. He was once elected as the Mayor of Klerksdorp. Johanna was always by his side. She was a devoted mother.

Kobus had other siblings as well. They were 7 kids, four brothers and three sisters. To name the brothers from the eldest Dawie, Johny, Kobus and Louis. The sisters were Kotie, Hantie and Maggie. Sadly Kotie and Hantie passed away. The boys leisure time consisted of bicycle rally competitions, cricket and rugby games etc. They lived nearby a park and the kids from the neighbouring suburbs often visited.

When John sold their home and moved to Viljoen Street nr 13, in the same suburb, he invited the youngsters from all over to compete in some traditional activity (Boeresport) The place of interest was just opposite their new home. Dawie was the brother who build a haunted house to keep the kids busy. He developed the skills to be a magician.

John often invited people of the community to visit. The visitors were well known and skilled people like doctors, lawyers etc.

Hantie and Dawie were guitarist and formed a band with other youngsters to play for a couple of events. Kobus would discover what his hidden talents were very soon.

CHAPTER 2

The Boyhood Dream

A s for a young kid of 12 there were a lot of choices to do in his leisure time. Kobus loved to developed the skills to be a good rugby player. He was physical in good shape and convinced himself to become better.

He played from an early age for his Primary School, which was Laerskool President in Klerksdorp. Rugby would become a major part of his life until 1983 when he had an injury while practising and had to give it up permanently. Between 1973 and 1983 he played for several Rugby clubs such as Westelikes, Strathvaal and President Brand's Club. He played Provincial rugby later after military service. Always as a scrum half. He also played cricket.

The thing that kept his attention was to do all kinds of recordings. The aim was real radio dramas. At first he went to Dawkinsville where the mine dunes could be found. Most of the kids enjoyed it to slide down and play for hours at a time. It was there that Kobus did his first official recordings. Just next to the dunes there were cattle as well. He recorded their activities.

When his great, great grandfather used to live with them, the family gathered in the lounge one day. That was the time that the box type Radio was a household item throughout South Africa. Kobus hid behind the Radio and started to broadcast spontaneously. His great, great grandfather was a captain in the Anglo-Boer War, captain John would be mentioned on 'real radio'.

In the 70's there was a SABC Radio Drama on air which was named "Die Wildtemmer". One particular character was named Ting Tong. Kobus called the SABC and asked if he could send an audio tape in. It was about imitating the well known character. He then did send the recording to the SABC. Francois van Heynegen invited him to visit the SABC. Francois told him that he never heard a voice so similar as to the original voice.

It was then and there that the seed to broadcast was planted and would become a reality.

CHAPTER 3

As for every business the requirement for a vision is a reality. In Radio Business one of the most important objectives will be to educate, inform and entertain people. To have a business plan for at least two years ahead is also very important. This vision however was a bit different.

Before we went on air for the first time, the prayer in Kobus's heart was that the Lord would open the door to broadcast. In every cell group gathering we prayed and asked for His will. Amandelbult Mine where we resided was 20 minutes drive to Thabazimbi. Every morning Kobus would stretch out his hand and asked the Lord for guidance and answers.

An evangelistic calling on your life which meant praying for and serve people was part of life. On two different mines where Kobus was working he arranged for services to be held within the hostels for the workers. It was Hartebeesfontein Mine situated in Stilfontein as well as Vaal Reefs near Orkney in North West. He appointed an interpreter to minister to the people. First the sermon and then the altar call. Hundreds attended the services. He even bought his own tent to minister to people but sold it later. The money to purchase the tent was sponsored by someone.

The Vision with a difference was a reality as much as the business plan for 2 years ahead. If there would only be one person saved it all be worth a while. The thought of climb unto a high mountain and preach the gospel would become a reality.

When we started broadcasting back in 2008, the response was overwhelming. People from all church denominations called after the program. Sometimes it was just for an encouraging prayer. Other times for healing etc.

It was indeed an alternative Vision for a Radio Business. Kobus kept his faith and trusted Abba for this dream.

CHAPTER 4

Kroonpark / Radio Panorama

We became friends with Chris and Mary-Ann Loots when we were residing in the Village Amandelbult.

In 2002 we visit Margate, which is situated on the South Coast of South Africa. It was in December and there were lots of visitors. We booked at Skippers which was a haven for holiday visitors. The food was excellent and there was a swimming pool in the centre of the complex, a pool table, darts and table tennis to keep us occupied in the evenings. There was a flea market as well. We also visited the Snake- and Bird Parks in the vicinity. The kids loved the beach and canoeing on the lagoon. There were also artists that entertained the holiday visitors. Cellphone companies organised some events there during the festive seasons and holidays.

We visit Oribi Gorge which is one of South Africa's wonders and awe striking. We had a ride on a local train between the local towns on the South Coast.

We visit the Kine's to watch one of Leon Schuster's latest movies.

While we enjoyed our stay in Margate, we planned our Festive Season. We decided to hire two caravans and stay at Kroonpark.

On the 23rd December 2002 we arrived there. Kroonpark was an upper class holiday resort At the resort there was a heated swimming pool, splashed pool, mini golf, super tube, and amphitheatre. There were also luxury chalets available for accomodation There were a lot of barbecue facilities as well. At the caravan park there were ablution blocks, laundry and scullery tubs, washing machines and driers.

While we visited Kroonpark we could tune into a local Community Radio Station (Radio Panorama which is near Hennenman in the Free State). They broadcast 24 hours a day, 7 days a week in Afrikaans and English. It features music, entertainment and information.

As we sat there listening, the reality hit us that there is a need in our Community for such a Radio Station. If that could materialize the Boyhood dream would become a reality. From thereon that was the topic of discussion.

When we arrived back in Amandelbult, we started to pray for this specific request and if that be in the will of our Father, that it may come to life.

CHAPTER 5

Application For Licence

After a fantastic festive season we headed home with the dream that was crystal clear. The work to obtain a broadcasting Licence would start.

In January 2003 Kobus registered a Company named Radio Bushveld. He then contacted the Independent Communication Authority (ICASA) of South Africa which regulates broadcasting. They always ensure affordable services of a high quality to all South Africans. In terms of Section 31.1 of the electronic communication a person may transmit any signal by radio and in accordance with the Radio frequency spectrum licence. The Application forms had to be downloaded from the internet, filled in and send back to Icasa. It has been time consuming because the only time the administration could be done was in the evenings. Kobus worked as a plumber and later as a clerk of works at Amandelbult Section (Anglo America) during the day. The relevant information for the applicant was program schedule, broadcasting area, languages such as Afrikaans, English and Setswana. Representing of employees (diversity). The equipment to be used should be Icasa type approved. Would the studio be wheelchair friendly?

While Kobus was busy with the application we had a yearly festival in Thabazimbi called the "Wildfees". Every year it was a big event for such a small town. Some of the well known artists attended the festival and needless to say the people enjoyed it. In 2005 we hired a caravan to be present on the premises. We had to get 3000 signatures to confirm that there was indeed a need for another Radio Station, this time a Community Radio Station. There were already RSG, Radio Pretoria and Jacaranda which is a Commercial Radio Station. We worked during the festival and in the end got our signatures.

In 2008 the requirement was 20 copies of the Application. It should be handed in on a specific date and time. I remember it very well. We were invited to attend a festival in Witbank (nowadays eMalahleni) during the Easter Weekend. During that weekend Hennie Smit supported us with some of the admin. We also met a guy named

Hansie which encouraged us as well. He did some of the outstanding printing for us. He also said a prayer with us if it will be the Father's will, the application would be granted. We met Victor Grootboom from Icasa at the festival as well. He told us that if we will comply with all of Icasa's rules, we will get a broadcasting Licence.

On the Monday (D-day) when we were on our way to Icasa's office, I was still putting documents together and bind some of the copies. It has been nerve-wrecking. We made it 10 minutes before closing time.

Kobus left Sandton, the area where Icasa's office is situated with a prayer in his heart. Now the wait was on.

CHAPTER 6

The Buzz / Radio Bushveld

I remember a time when we were sponsored with a brand new mixer. Though small, we felt spoiled and it came in very handy. To add a laptop and two microphones was the first real step in the broadcasting Industry. Kobus's boyhood dream would slowly but surely become a reality. He first registered an internet radio station and ran some gospel programs during the day. In the evenings he tested the first waters of real broadcasting and from the start was a natural behind the microphone.

Icasa (The Independent Communications Authority of South Africa) contacted us in May 2008 and had good news. The application to broadcast had been approved and the due date was the 1st June 2008.

We felt blessed and hire our local Show Grounds for the opening of Radio Bushveld. Hennie Smit with the whole team of Radio Kragbron attend the opening. On the opening day Hennie congratulated us with everything and promised us his continuous support for the years to come. Hennie van Rensburg, Maggie May, Victor van Wyk and some of our local artists entertained us on that day. Franco Loots who later became a presenter took a video of the events on that day. Many of our local people attended the event.

There was an ideal shop available to rent and the renovations started. With the financial support of my brother Peet Cilliers, which was a five figure amount, we build one studio to broadcast. A space where the sound engineers could work, two offices, a kitchen and a reception area. It felt like a big accomplishment.

There were a lot of people interested that would become part of the Radio Bushveld team. Hennie Smit was the Manager of Radio Kragbron at that time. He had many years of experience in TV and Radio and confirmed that he will help us in every possible way. Johan Brits, who was also a well known presenter in South Africa, asked the presenters to read a news bulletin in Afrikaans, our native language. I personally think news readers must be born for this special task. Johan Brits also teached us to visualize an environment when broadcasting, to be careful not to present in a monotone voice and to use humor carefully. He also stressed the fact that we must always look for interesting news locally and internationally to share with the listeners.

The rest of the team which was appointed, received training for sound engineering, program scheduling and administration.

Victor van Wyk who worked for Anglo America and was a software designer for many years, was appointed as a Station Manager.

We were officialy ready to broadcast. A new unique voice would be heard in the beautiful Bushveld.

CHAPTER 7

On the 1st June 2008, Radio's Bushveld's doors opened. It was a milestone after working so hard to get a licence and comply with Icasa's requirements. Kobus first tested the waters. He was and still is a natural presenter. As from our first date I told him that he has a beautiful voice.

Franco Loots showed an interest to become a presenter. As he studied multi media for five years the position suited him very well. He was bright as has a perfect voice for radio. Currently we ask him to do recordings for new advertisements. His father was a preacher and lived with much humor. Franco has a similar personality. On this specific day he was present and asked the people to call and confirm where they could hear us. People from all over our broadcasting area phoned and confirm that they could listen to Radio Bushveld.

Me and Debbie Viljoen also stop by. She studied communication at Technicon in South Africa. The presenter position also suited her very well. Later other presenters came to visit. I remember how nervous most of the presenters were to broadcast for the first time.

The first Saturday after our doors opened, people from the community were invited to say hallo and have something to eat. We had a guest book where people could sign and leave a message. We were stunned at first by the heart warming reaction of the community. That evening we blessed the old age home with food. It felt that we belonged.

We started with our regular programs. Franco Loots did the breakfast show which was named "Die wrede wakker word". Kobus and a co-presenter did a program called "Die Kletsers" which became very popular due to humor and upbeat Afrikaans music. The listeners could send requests in during the program.

I talked to our Pastor Steven Enslin, which we appointed as liaison officer, to do a program just after he will finished his. He talked about relationships and the program became well known. My idea was a program with beautiful poems and quotes. It was called "Liebe Dich", meaning I love you in English. The music add value to the program as it consisted of most hit songs which was suitable for a late night show. The time schedule was 22h00 – 23h00 at night.

Though every presenter had to deal with some critics, we started well. Later me and one of the most talented presenters Verena Jackson, started a program called "Books and Magazines Galore" We interviewed many South African Authors.

Kobus started a gospel program on a Sunday between 12h00 and 13h00. Many times after the program finished, people called and asked him to pray with them for a specific request.

We implemented many other programs like a Country program, Classical program, a community program with Debbie Viljoen. Jessy Lang which is now a presenter at Overvaal Stereo 96.1Fm, did a program for kids in the morning. Marie Steenekamp did a medical program and invited all the doctors in our community to participate. We also syndicated a gardening program with Lichvaal Stereo 92.6Fm in Lichtenburg. The preachers from different denominations, came to do a program when Jessy Lang finished.

Tobie Lombaard, previously a journalist started a program for people to send song requests and messages. It became very popular. He presented the program both on Friday and Saturday evenings. Elias Molemale and Pearle did Setswana educational programs as well. We supported Elias to get his own broadcasting licence and is the proud Licencee Holder of Kgatleng Fm 91.3. Recently it showed on the BRCF statistics that they have 33 000 listeners on Fm.

We were thankful that everything went smooth. There were a lot of advertisers that came on board. Anglo America sponsored us with a R200 000.00 donation.

We ran a competition with our local Spar and many people entered. One of the big events in Thabazimbi is the yearly Marakele National Park's marathon. We did a live broadcast from there. The Park is the second largest in South Africa (67 000 hectares).

The listeners spoiled us with presents, traditional South African food such as "braaivleis" and "melktert". A lady from Rooiberg gave us a dining set. which we still use on a daily basis.

We ran a program later which was called "Ruil & Bie" where listeners could sell or exchange something. It became very popular.

A lady named Wally advertised puppies and gave us one. We named him Krummel because he is so small.

We were in need of some more music, since we just started broadcasting and the listeners spoiled us with lots of cd's.

I had a Christian friend and she often spoiled me with lunch. One day she spoiled me and paid for a sauna. We made friends for life in the Radio Industry. One couple was Dries and Ans from the farm Klein Elandsfontein. We often visit them and experienced the simplicity of life there. They were humble but loving people.

In 2009 Hennie Smit from Radio Kragbron blessed us with an outside broadcasting vehicle, we even named him Skillie.

Radio Bushveld became a very popular Radio Station in Thabazimbi and surrounding areas. Some of the listeners had three radios in their households. One in the kitchen, one in the bedroom and one in the garden, all tuned to 104.9Fm.

We met and interviewed many famous people. The ones I will remember was the Country singers of South Africa Barbara Ray, Billy Forest, Clive Bruce, Bobby Angel. One of South Africa's biggest celebrities Steve Hofmeyr signed our guest book. We had two interviews with him about books he wrote. In 2008 he wrote a book "Mense van my Asem" which sold 50 000 copies. In 2020 mid lockdown we interviewed him about his book "Die Kwesbares". We interviewed the due Mad Mike and Mark from a well known TV Program. I once communicated with Dr. Caroline Leaf who is a well known author and communication pathologist and cognitive neuroscientist to have an interview. We still have to schedule it someday which we are looking forward to.

We will forever remember the good times with Radio Bushveld. It was the first step to enrich our lives and make a difference in the Community.

CHAPTER 8

Tough Times

After the initial buzz, decline in business started to show due to a couple of reasons. There were other directors on the board which dominated everything, like making decisions that was not well thought over.

There was a guy who was manager at a previous radio station, who was appointed as a new station manager. Victor van Wyk was yet to be removed and appointed as marketing manager. We said let's wait for the appointment for several reasons, but in the end it happened anyway. Some of the well known programs came to an end immediately and new programs have been implemented. It has been the wrong choice. Most of our advertisers stopped their advertisements and payments.

Radio involvement had always come with some strings attached through the years. No matter place and time. We were nothing different. For first time presenters, after training, broadcasting was a haven. Fame was the equivalent of addiction to opium. Not every presenter could balance their lives. There were competition, jealousy, even gossiping amongst the presenters. Some of the people from the community made it part of their lives to come in and gossip about us on a daily basis.

There was a presenter involved who even called the Mine security and tell them anonymously to check out our house because Kobus was stealing some of the Mines stuff. My daughter was at home for the holiday when the mine security arrived at nine to check everything out. Kobus didnt know about anything when the people called him and tell him he must drive to our home. At the end they couldn't find anything.

Another incident happened afterwards. A part of Kobus duties was to inspect houses when people moved out. One day there was a 500ml full of a kind of platinum left at one empty house worth a million South African Rand. We saw that as a trap. Kobus brought it home and as we didn't know really what it was, we called the Mine Security. They wrote a declaration and even accused Kobus of not being honest.

There were people obsessed to own the Radio Station. We have never known such meanness in life. As we were watching TV one Friday evening, a car stopped at our house. One of the guys thought we were in the main room and threw a large brick and we only heard the glass shattering. Our neighbour's rushed out and asked if we were ok? One of the directors and another presenter even asked people from the community to protest against us for some "issues" they had against us. Nobody but them were present that evening. No one of the Community supported them.

All what was going on was creating tension between me and Kobus. The rest of the Board, some who didnt invest even R10.00 into the business dictated him all the time. One morning I have had enough of everything. I called Kobus and tell him to come home that we can discuss everything and try to find a solution for our problems. At the end I told him I want to go on my own. I packed and was on my way to Rustenburg. At that stage we were battling financially. My daughter, now a teacher was in her second year studying B-ed. We put all our savings and money we received from my brother into the business. My plan was to go to Potchefstroom to people that were like our own parents for support. I stopped at a pawn shop and sold my overlocker to at least have money for petrol and food. I thought of my freedom and how I will manage my life for the future. I arrived late in the City and decided to spend the night in the car. It was winter and bitterly cold. I did pack some warm clothes. That night I was in an all low emotional state. I have had enough of all the gossiping, the financial problems and the politics in business. I felt safe where I was parking. That was at a well known garage with a restaurant in Rustenburg. I realised that night how easily people sell drugs. Also how many people are traveller's and live in their cars full time. There was a guy and his girlfriend next to me who told me to stay there for the night then I will be safe. I gave him a cd and told me about salvation, though my own life was in turmoil. That evening Kobus told me he will resign from the mine if I don't come back. That was a big decision for me to make because of my daughter's studies. I decided to go home and find a solution. I remember the feeling of having a home instead of living in a car. Sleeping in a warm bed with enough blankets. Have warm water available for a bath or shower and was thankful.

Shortly after that Kobus told me he will disband the Board because of all the turmoil their decisions had bring into the business. Not one of them had any experience of running a radio business, but they thought they know it all.

The salaries of the personell was paid with an overdraft. When business was decreasing, the manager of a bank change that to a personal loan. At the end to make matters worst, we didn't once saw the Summons. The Bailiff arrived at our home. We were so shocked about everything and arranged to find a solution with our lawyers. At the end we were in debt with a six figure amount. We have to closed our office doors as well. All the debt, we were liable for. It included telephone, water and lights, the internet etc. That was the worst humiliation of our lives and our trust in people was rock buttom.

We owned Sentech our signal distribution a lot of money and we couldn't pay them. They cut off our signal as well. Once famous and known by most of the people we were on our own, with the exception of two people who stood by us. Bancrupt and ashamed were us then. No minister, pastor or anyone from the community came to visit us. Up to now I can recall that difficult time. Kobus decided that from the start, he will keep his job on the mine for stability. He had to deal with the shame and humiliation and didn't talk to me about how he felt. We were married 25 years then.

We had to deal with the financial impact of the loss and the rest of our expenses. I didn't deal with it very good and fall into a deep depression. I lost complete trust in humanity. My thoughts were that animals are better than people. We lost all our friends of 25 years because of Radio. I was lonely and often visit my previous neighbor. She didn't even gave me water to drink. When we lived as neighbour's, she often asked me for money and favours, in which I was always helpful.

Although she was a Penti-costal lady, she wouldn't listen to my complaints and I was heartbroken. I just needed someone to listen to me. Until today I will carry that experience with me. In the end I thought that the only hope and trust will be in faith and God and worked on that.

I realize that if you know the Bible better, you would have understand human behaviour better. As for the King of Kings, Jesus had gone through much more humiliation than us, and choose to forgive. So did we afterwards and became winners in the end.

CHAPTER 9

Faith In Action

Words are powerful. When the words we speak is in accordance to His word, His power is released. After so many disappointments and mistrust in people, it was time to focus on our personal lives. What we didn't realize then, was that we had so many good things ahead of us. Firstly our daughter was in her second year at the North West University and she could apply for a study loan. One of our South African Banks funded her studies and we were so grateful. She then finished her honours in Education in 2013. Anglo America subsidies his workers with housing. We were fortunate to live in a D2 house. It was usually granted to engineers, but we had that luxury. The house also consisted of an extra study room. We were surprised that the mine decided that our house was on the list to be upgraded. They replaced the tiles, painted the house and upgraded our barbecue area. They also replaced our stove, with a luxury one. It looked beautiful and we felt a bit spoiled. Once our studio in town was closed due to high rental, we plan to broadcast from home for the time being.

One morning Kobus got a call from someone regarding galvanize steel and if he wasn't interested to buy it. He purchased it and asked someone with a low bed to pick it up, and keep it on the guys farm for a while. The same guy made us an offer for the steel and yes we were on our way to recover financially. We resell the steel for an excellent amount and we purchased a new broadcast transmitter from the UK. As our broadcasting licence was still valid, we started to broadcast from home. On the day that the transmitter arrived at Oliver Tambo airport, Kobus had to pay R4 000.00 import tax. He was at the bank and somebody sponsored him with the needed amount.

That was also the first time a presenter from the UK approached us to do a program on our Station. Andy Sim is well known and his program across the mercy can be heard on several radio stations around the globe. It was during that time that the name of the Radio Station has been changed from Thaba Stereo 104.9Fm to Waterberg Stereo 104.9Fm. It seemed practical to do the change, as we broadcast in the Waterberg Region, Limpopo, South Africa. We also changed the logo of the Company.

We applied for funding at the MDDA and had to await the outcome. In our personal lives we always believed in praying even fasting for a specific thing. In this case it was that the funding might be approved.

We always aim to stay positive, no matter what. By then we knew that Abba Father would supply to all our needs according to His riches and glory.

CHAPTER 10

Seven Figure Sponsorship

We applied twice before for funding from the MDDA and both times it was declined. We thought maybe if we try once again, it might be a case of third time lucky.

The saying third time lucky might sometimes be true. In our case, it surely has been. After officially retiring at Anglo American we hoped that the funding from the MDDA might be approved. It was part of our planning to stay in the beautiful Bushveld where the climate envites the people to never leave. We have only 4 months winter in South Africa and in Thabazimbi most of the winter days are sunny. It is not yet a City and all the shops are close to each other. You occasionally need to drive to the nearby Cities in need of something.

One sunny Saturday morning we were on our way to Pretoria Gauteng, to visit our daughter, when the phone rang. It was Kabelo who was our representative from the MDDA. He said Kobus I have good news for you. Your application has been approved for a seven figure amount (R2 000 000). Kobus was over the moon with the outcome and we could plan ahead for the next eighteen months.

Kabelo visited us to discuss how the money would be spend. The budget consisted of rental, salaries for 5 people, internet and telephone costs. That amount should be spend in cash. The rest of the money had been allocated for microphones, computers, all the technical equipment necessary for broadcasting and office chairs. They also paid for sound proof equipment like carpets and boards for the walls. We felt blessed with the fancy small speakers that could be put even in the roof of the building. We also received two air conditioners and two flat screen televisions.

We could keep on broadcasting and would face the day to day challenges again. All honor to our Abba Father who always did and always will do miraculous things and open doors.

CHAPTER 11

2017 - Present

Kobus was now officially on pension and could devote all his time to Waterberg Stereo 104.9Fm. With the sponsoring from the MDDA we could manage to hire yet another building to broadcast. It was twice the size of our previous studio. We build our new studios. One for broadcasting and the other for recordings. One guy who used to visit us said it look impressive. One of our dentists words were I'm taking my hat off to you.

After the difficulties of the last couple of years, it felt that we could yet make the next step in the business world. This time the Management has changed and we were ready for the challenges ahead. For the next two years we were covered for rental, salaries, telephone and internet by the MDDA. The ghost of the past was still there. We had to learn to be successful in marketing and management. The first two years 2017 and 2018 has been a big challenge. After the history of Thaba Stereo 104.9Fm, the people was hesitant to advertise, but we kept our faith. On one occasion a guy came by and ask us to do an advert but we decline due to personal view. The amount was R4 000.00 and we really could have used that money wisely.

As we already had a studio in Modimolle we planned to open a studio in Lephalale as well. This town is approximately 130kms from Thabazimbi and it was a perfect opportunity. When we applied for a licence way back, Icasa approved gap fillers for Modimolle, Lephalale and Bela Bela which is also 130kms away. The frequencies that was approved, was Thabazimbi, Lephalale and Modimolle.

We started the marketing in Lephalale in 2019 and fortunately signed some new clients. We enjoyed mixing fun and marketing. I practiced golf one day and enjoyed it. We were invited to join our marketing lady one evening at a pub and grill. We had so much fun. The owner of the business is a good chef and a singer as well. I asked him if I could sing one song with him and he accept. Somewhere Between was a nice Country song to do. It was contagious. Kobus then sang an Afrikaans song Transkaroo. Thereafter our marketing ladies husband sang Soos Bloed. We played pool and I was the champion. Needless to say we have not had an experience like that in a very long time.

When Covid 19 came, our plans for opening a studio was put on hold. Though the pandemic affected lots of businesses, we could kept our doors open with large subsidy from the South African Government. As we felt a decrease in our income, we planned to move to a cheaper premises to rent. In 2020 in November we started at our third studio for half the rent.

Early in 2021 we were approached by a Media Company to apply for a subsidy from Microsoft. It was to create an App for Waterberg Steteo 104.9Fm. It took us about two weeks to did the Paper work. Sometimes late at night and in the end it was approved. The Sponsorship was a six figure amount (R300 000) and we were so thankful. The App can be downloaded for free by anyone who are interested to listen to our Radio Station. Every potential listener must register and can then send messages, requests and listen to our podcasts.

We upgraded our new studio in May 2022, and feel very blessed. We also celebrated 14 years in business on the 1st June 2022. Currently we have Million Dollar Companies which agreed in partnering with us. Our goal is to keep serving our Community. We are grateful that we could support an organisation named Feed the Poor for a couple of years with funds, school clothes, blankets and back to school vouchers. We also donated masks and sanitizers in the Covid 19 hard lockdown in South Africa.

As for now we will always live with humbleness and faith. Faith is our ever present companion in business and in our personal life.

CHAPTER 12

Faith, Hope
And Passion

Whether in our personal lives or business environment, we learned that faith is everything. Faith had become the foundation and we would not compromise whatsoever. We learned from many years back to put our trust in Abba Father. He is and will always be Jehovah Jireh, our Provider. With hard work and hope for the future any business can survive, even after failure.

Passion is the necessary thing to make your dreams a reality. Go get your dream.

Epilogue

If you can dream it, you can do it. Although we had and still have many challenges ahead, we aim to live day by day. We were never promised that only good days exist. Some days are diamonds, some days are stones as one famous singer used to sing.

History can tell how many people lost it all and started from scratch. The business world is all about risks and riches.

Faith will never lose its power. Believing and trusting our Heavenly Father, made a big difference in people lives all around the globe.

He will always be the Lover of my soul.

Lightning Source UK Ltd.
Milton Keynes UK
UKHW021052121222
413783UK00010B/87